CHRISTMAS CRACK-UPS

Amanda Li is a writer and editor who has worked in children's publishing for many years. She lives in London, England, with her family.

Q: What sits at her desk, arranges her pens and pencils, gets up to make coffee and eat a banana, returns to her desk, listens to the radio, and illustrates joke books?

A: Jane Eccles!

Amanda Li

CHRISTMAS CRACK-UPS

BURSTING WITH FESTIVE FUNNY STUFF

Illustrated by Jane Eccles

KINGFISHER
NEW YORK

"Especially for my beloved Beak"—J. E.

KINGFISHER
LONDON & NEW YORK

Text copyright © Kingfisher 2010
Illustrations copyright © Jane Eccles 2009
Published in the United States by Kingfisher,
175 Fifth Ave., New York, NY 10010
Kingfisher is an imprint of Macmillan Children's Books, London.

Distributed in the U.S. by Macmillan, 175 Fifth Ave., New York, NY 10010
Distributed in Canada by H.B. Fenn and Company Ltd., 34 Nixon Road,
Bolton, Ontario L7E 1W2

Library of Congress Cataloging-in-Publication data
has been applied for.

ISBN: 978-0-7534-3045-3

Kingfisher books are available for special promotions and premiums.
For details contact: Special Markets Department, Macmillan, 175 Fifth Ave.,
New York, NY 10010.

For more information, please visit www.kingfisherbooks.com

Printed and bound in the U.K. by CPI Mackays, Chatham ME5 8TD
1 3 5 7 9 8 6 4 2
0710

What's red and white and goes up and down and up and down?

Santa Claus stuck in an elevator.

What's red and white, bounces, and goes, "Ho ho ho"?

Santa on a pogo stick.

Why didn't Santa Claus get wet when he lost his umbrella?

It wasn't raining.

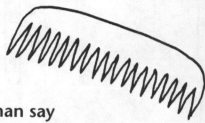

What did the bald man say when he got a comb for Christmas?

"Thanks, I'll never part with it."

Knock, knock.
Who's there?
Rabbit.
Rabbit who?
Rabbit up neatly, it's a present.

Why did the elf curl up in the fireplace?

He wanted to sleep like a log.

Where do you find elves?

Depends on where you left them.

Oh, there you are!

What's the best key to get at Christmas?

A turkey.

What leads you to the Christmas presents in police stations?

Santa Clues.

Who brings Christmas presents to baby sharks?

Santa Jaws.

What squeaks and is scary?

The Ghost of Christmouse Past.

What does Frosty the Snowman wear on his head?

An ice cap.

Why does Santa Claus go down the chimney on Christmas Eve?

Because it soots him.

What happens when Frosty the Snowman gets dandruff?

He gets snowflakes.

Who carries all of Santa's books?

His books elf.

What do reindeer always say before telling you a joke?

"This one will sleigh you."

Which of Santa's reindeer need to mind his manners the most?

Rude-olph.

What does Frosty the Snowman eat for lunch?

Icebergers.

What does Frosty the Snowman like to put on his icebergers?

Chilly sauce.

What do sheep say to each other at Christmastime?

"Merry Christmas to ewe."

What's red and white and red and white and red and white?

Santa Claus rolling down a hill.

On which side of Santa's face is his beard?

The outside.

What nationality are Santa and Mrs. Claus?

North Polish.

What kind of bills do elves have to pay?

Jingle bills.

What did one angel say to the other angel?

"Halo there."

Pizza Fit for a King

Good King Wenceslas looked out his window at the thick snow. It was too cold to go outside, and he was feeling very hungry. Suddenly he had a great idea. He would order a pizza and get it delivered! Quickly he made the call and ordered himself a large cheese and tomato pizza.

"How would you like it?" asked the pizza delivery boy.

"Deep pan, crisp, and even!" replied Good King Wenceslas.

What happens if you eat the Christmas decorations?

You get tinsellitis.

What two things should you never eat before breakfast on Christmas Day?

Lunch and dinner.

Who is never hungry at Christmas?

The turkey—he's always stuffed.

Why do bakers work so hard at Christmas?

Because they need the dough.

What is 20 feet tall, has sharp teeth, and goes, "Ho ho ho"?

Tyranno-santa rex!

Why did Santa's helper float away?

He ate elf-rising flour.

What has a trunk and is found at the North Pole?

A lost elephant.

What did the Christmas stocking say when it had a hole in it?

"Well, I'll be darned!"

Dad: Would you like a pocket calculator for Christmas?

Dennis: No, thanks. I already know how many pockets I have.

What do you call a boy trying to get the creases out of his clothes at the North Pole?

Brrrr-ian.

Martin: Why did your dad get splinters from the book you gave him for Christmas?

Mervin: It was a logbook.

17

Man in store: I'm trying to buy a Christmas present for my wife. Can you help me out?

Store assistant: Certainly, sir. Which way did you come in?

Mrs. Tubby: I want to buy a nice Christmas cake, please.

Confectioner: This is a nice one.

Mrs. Tubby: It looks to me as if mice have been nibbling it.

Confectioner: Oh no, that's impossible.

Mrs. Tubby: How can you be so sure?

Confectioner: Because the cat's been lying on it all day.

What do vampires sing on New Year's Eve?

Auld fang syne.

Why didn't the skeleton go to the New Year's Eve party?

He had no body to go with.

Why is a turkey like an imp?

Because it's always a-gobblin'.

What jumps from cake to cake and tastes like almonds?

Tarzipan.

Where do snowmen dance?

At snowballs.

What did Mrs. Claus say to Santa Claus?

"It looks like rain, dear."

What can Santa give away and still keep?

A cold.

If Santa Claus and Mrs. Claus had a child, what would he be called?

A subordinate clause.

Where is the best place to put your Christmas tree?

Between your Christmas two and your Christmas four.

Why did the reindeer cross the road?

Because he was tied to a chicken.

What do you get if you cross an apple with a Christmas tree?

A pineapple.

A boy went to the butcher shop and saw that the turkeys were 90 cents a pound. He asked the butcher, "Do you raise them yourself?"

"Of course I do," the butcher replied. "They were only fifty cents a pound this morning!"

How do you tell the difference between canned turkey and canned cranberries?

Read the labels.

Elf: Santa, the reindeer swallowed my pencil. What should I do?
Santa: Use a pen.

Where was Santa when the lights went out?

In the dark.

What do you get if you cross a bell with a skunk?

Jingle smells.

What does Frosty the Snowman drink?

Iced tea.

How long should an elf's legs be?

Just long enough to reach the ground.

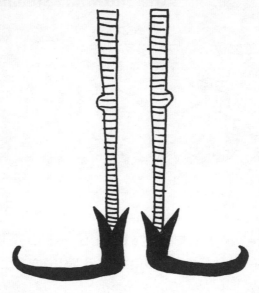

Who is Frosty the Snowman's favorite aunt?

Aunt Arctica.

How does Frosty the Snowman get around?

On an ice-icle.

What did the police officer say when he saw Frosty the Snowman stealing?

"Freeze!"

If athletes get athlete's foot, what do Santa's elves get?

Mistle-toes.

What do they call a wild elf in Texas?

Gnome on the range.

How did Rudolph learn to read?

He was elf-taught.

What did the elf say when he was teaching Santa Claus to use the computer?

"First, yule log in!"

What do ghosts put on their turkey at Christmas?

Grave-y.

There once was a Viking named Rudolph the Red. He was at home one day with his wife. He looked out the window and said, "Look, darling, it's raining."

She shook her head. "I don't think so, dear. I think it's snowing."

But Rudolph knew better, so he said, "Let's go outside and we'll find out."

They went outside and discovered that it was in fact raining. And Rudolph turned to his wife and said, "I knew it was raining. Rudolph the Red knows rain, dear!"

Knock, knock.
Who's there?
Wenceslas.
Wenceslas who?
Wenceslas bus home on Christmas Eve?

Why do people cry at Christmastime?

Because they are santa-mental.

What did the snowman's wife give him when she was angry with him?

The cold shoulder.

What do you get if you cross a shark with a snowman?

Frostbite.

Knock, knock.
Who's there?
Mary.
Mary who?
Mary Christmas!

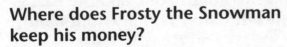

Where does Frosty the Snowman keep his money?

In a snow bank.

**What does Santa use
when he goes fishing?**

His North Pole.

**What falls down all the time at the
North Pole but never hurts itself?**

Snow.

**If I'm standing at the North Pole,
facing the South Pole, and the east is
on my left, what's on my right hand?**

Fingers.

Where does a ten-foot-tall polar bear sleep?

Anywhere it wants to.

How do rabbits travel home for Christmas?

By hare plane.

AIR

Knock, knock.
Who's there?
Holly.
Holly who?
Holly-days are here again!

Why was Santa's little helper depressed?
He had low elf-esteem.

What's the best thing to put into your Christmas dinner?
Your teeth.

What did Adam tell his girlfriend on December 24?

"It's Christmas, Eve."

What does Tarzan sing at Christmastime?

Jungle Bells.

Why do elves scratch themselves?

Because they're the only ones who know where they itch.

What do angry mice send each other in December?

Cross-mouse cards.

WAITING ROOM

Why did the Christmas cake go to the doctor?

Because he was feeling crummy.

What time does a duck wake up on Christmas morning?

At the quack of dawn.

Why are Christmas trees like bad knitters?

They both drop their needles!

Who delivers Christmas presents to dogs?

Santa Paws.

Mother: Why are you crying?
Samantha: Jennifer broke my Christmas doll.
Mother: How did she do that?
Samantha: I hit her over the head with it.

What do elves learn in school?

The elf-abet.

What goes, "Ho Ho Swoosh! Ho Ho Swoosh!"?

Santa in a revolving door.

Where does Santa stay when he's on vacation?

At a ho-ho-hotel!

Why does Santa Claus owe everything to the elves?

Because he is an elf-made man.

What's red and white and gives presents to gazelles?

Santelope.

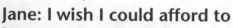

Jane: I wish I could afford to buy a pedigreed puppy for Christmas.

Wayne: Why do you want a pedigreed puppy?

Jane: Oh, I don't want one. I just wish I had enough money to buy one.

What does Frosty the Snowman take when he gets sick?

A chill pill.

What goes, "Oh oh oh"?

Santa Claus walking backward!

43

What do you call a little lobster who won't share his Christmas toys?

Shellfish.

Lizzie: Mom, do you remember that plate Grandma gave you last Christmas that you were so worried we might break?

Mother: Yes.

Lizzie: Well, your worries are over.

What's a wise bird's favorite Christmas carol?

Owl Be Home for Christmas.

Ben: Did you like the dictionary I gave you for Christmas?

Ken: Yes, I've been trying to find the words to thank you.

What kind of ball doesn't bounce?

A snowball.

How does Rudolph know when Christmas is coming?

He looks at his calen-deer.

What kind of cake does Frosty the Snowman like?

Any kind, as long as it has lots of icing.

What do you call an elf who steals gift wrap from the rich and gives it to the poor?

Ribbon Hood.

What does Santa get if he's stuck in a chimney?

Claustrophobic.

**What's the best present for
someone who likes to play it cool?**

A combined refrigerator and CD player.

Gemma: First the good news—Mom gave me a goldfish for Christmas.

Emma: What's the bad news?

Gemma: I get the bowl next Christmas.

Why did Santa spring back up the chimney?

To try out his new jumpsuit.

"Thanks for the electric guitar you gave me for Christmas," Timmy said to his uncle. "It's the best present I've ever got."

"That's great," said his uncle. "Do you know how to play it?"

"Oh, I don't play it. My mom gives me seven dollars a week not to play it during the day, and my dad gives me five dollars a week not to play it at night!"

Who sings "Love Me Tender" and makes Christmas toys?

Santa's Elvis.

What game do four reindeer play in the back of a Volkswagen Beetle?

Squash.

What Christmas carol is popular in the desert?

O Camel Ye Faithful.

Shane: How are you doing with the guitar your dad gave you for Christmas?

Wayne: Oh, I threw it away.

Shane: Why did you do that?

Wayne: It had a hole in the middle.

Little Belinda was given a bottle of perfume and a recorder for Christmas. Her parents' rather pompous friends arrived for lunch the next day, and as the family sat down at the table, Belinda confided to them, "If you smell a little smell and hear a little noise, it's me."

David: Have you bought your grandmother's Christmas present yet, Susie?

Susie: No. I was going to get her a handkerchief, but I changed my mind.

David: Why?

Susie: I can't figure out what size her nose is.

Why is Santa's nose in the middle of his face?

Because it's the scenter.

What did the sheep say to the shepherd?

"Season's bleatings."

Dad: What do you have your eye on for Christmas?

Dennis: I have my eye on that shiny red bike in the store on Main Street.

Dad: Well, you'd better keep your eye on it, because you'll never get your bottom on it.

Mrs. Feather: How much are those teddy bears?

Store assistant: Nine dollars for the pair or five dollars for one.

Mrs. Feather: Here's four dollars—I'll have the other one.

Annie: What does Santa do in the summer?

Danny: He's a gardener.

Annie: How do you know that?

Danny: Because he's always saying,
"Hoe hoe hoe."

What's the best thing to give your parents at Christmas?

A list of everything you want.

56

What's green, covered with tinsel, and says, "Ribbet, ribbet"?

A mistle-toad.

What kind of coat does Santa wear when it's raining on Christmas Eve?

A wet one.

What's the best Christmas present?

Difficult to say, but a drum takes a lot of beating.

**What happened when Mrs. Claus
served soap flakes instead of
cornflakes for breakfast?**

Santa was so angry, he foamed at the mouth.

What happened when Santa's dog ate garlic?

His bark was worse than his bite.

What's the wettest animal in the world?

A rain-deer.

Why are reindeer such bad dancers?

They have two left feet.

What do you call a reindeer with no eyes?

No idea.

What do you call a reindeer with no eyes and no legs?

Still no idea.

Other titles in the **Sidesplitters**
series you might enjoy: